Waking Up In Dreams

§

The Collected Poems
of Roland Verfaillie

vol. 2

Copyright © 2010 Purple Onion Press
All rights reserved
Published by Purple Onion press
San Francisco, CA

Designed and produced by Sigmund Rich, Purple Onion Press

Other works by Roland Verfaillie published by Purple Onion Press:
The Ashley Dancers
The Lie (screenplay)
the book of job(s)
the second book of job(s)
Hill of Sorrow/Mountain of Joy (Collected Poems)

No part of this book may be reproduced, stored in a retrieval system, or transmitted in any form, by any means, including mechanical, electronic, recording, or otherwise, without written permission from the publisher.

Writers Guild of America, East, Inc.
Registration Number: I227803
Date Registered, April 27, 2011

Waking Up In Dreams
ISBN 978-0-978708-54-2

Contents   Page
>>>

Introduction   5-12

Dream Series:

Waking Up In Dreams   15-25
Fire and Ashes   26-33
Izmir Bazaar   34-41
Kapali Carsi   42-48
The Chamber of Dreams

Nature:

The Mariner's Course   51-65
Joshua Tree   66-70

The Lighter Side:

Pulp Fiction   72-73
Poet   74-77

Flesh & Blood
Beauty & Mathematics

Immortal Me   80-85
1.618   86-99

"Those who dream by day are cognizant of many things which escape those who only dream at night."

§ **Edgar Allan Poe,** *"Eleonora"*

Introduction

Waking Up In Dreams

Those of us who daydream may be accused of dreaming our lives away. But, perhaps our dreams are our lives; as we live them each day *and* night. How do you tell the difference? Because we theorize that continuity defines our waking state? And that the disjointed, seemingly chaotic dream state is therefore less real? Dreams may be prophetic; prophesying events yet to happen. They may be the mind's moral inquisitor trying to right wrongs or work through unresolved problems. Or it may simply be the brain's overused and overloaded neural circuitry closing down to clean house during a REM cycle.

No doubt, dreams fascinate me. I have them all the time. Yes, I mean day and night. I'll wager you do too. This book of poetry titled, "Waking Up In Dreams," is a celebration of our dreaming lives. And like people, places and things, dreams can be good or bad. Like some people, they may arrive uninvited. As a vehicle for unhampered travel, a dream can transport you to alien places where you may encounter the strangest of things. You decide how you wish to define them. The poems I've written provide a context for the dream; a context which resonates with the universal themes which inhabit our lives.

The dream is a hoarder of miscellaneous thoughts, ideas and images. It is a magnet of sorts; that attracts the rust deposits of over-used, unused and disconnected images. Unfortunately, dreams have a poor sorting system for the images and sensations which arise. The poem's achievement is in the creation of coherence and beauty from the raw images and the coarse and prickly sensations that steadily bombard us. The poet renders his art through evocative images set to rhythm, and verse.

Some professional dream researchers consider the dream to be a meme generator. The meme is a relatively new concept that identifies how ideas and beliefs are transmitted between people and groups. They provide an explanation as to how cultural ideas, symbols and practices are spread throughout society. Our genes, on the one hand, transmit our biological information. Memes, on the other, transmit idea and belief information. I believe that poetry functions to unify the two domains. The poem, like the dream, is the communication of symbolic reference writ shorthand. The poem is more organized and coherent than the dream. The dream may be forgotten upon waking. But the poem reminds us of the forgotten content of our dreams, and lets us apply meaning within the context of our - for better or worse - culture bound lives. The dream which is dreamt in the waking hours of our days provides an opportunity to make something new and original out of those old, tired conventions. The ones society has outgrown. And like the dream theory of cleaning house, perhaps the poets and the dreamers help do the job.

Life needs dreams - both sleeping and waking. Dreaming keeps it interesting. Dreaming is the wishing well from which we may raise the pail of dreams-come-true; showing us our limitless possibilities. Life needs poetry to promote that which lies dormant within our great potential. Poetry gives our dreams momentum throughout our waking hours. In the waking hours we can make our dreams come true.

A short work of prose precedes this poetry collection. It is a vision that I recently experienced while traveling abroad. I must confess my skepticism when it comes to writing about visions and other paranormal experiences. I don't particularly subscribe to these experiences as suggesting having lived a former life; in some other time before our present incarnation. I merely exhort their seeming authenticity because of the clarity with which they steal upon us. Like any lucid dream, they may come unbidden during sleep, or invited during our waking hours. In our waking hours we can conjure images, or experience them as rising to the surface from the depths of our deep unconscious. Generally this occurs under special circumstances. Circumstances such as in the trance of meditation, drug intoxication, fatigue, or deprivation. Again whether induced purposefully, caused by ingesting drugs, or brought on by stress, they are - for the time we experience them - real.

The one vision I describe is one of dozens I have had over a lifetime. It serves as an example of the lucidity that dreams can possess. Moreover, a shared vision is quite remarkable. A shared vision is, as the reference suggests, experienced simultaneously by two or more people whom after having the vision, share what happened. The remarkable piece derives from reporting shared, similar content. If I envision a horseman dressed in gray and thundering in my direction then stops short and hands me a written message, and my partner reports the same occurrence, isn't that remarkable? Not astounding proof of joined past lives, or twins on steroids…just very, very interesting. I've had far fewer of this variety. So it is why I share one of them with you. It is also an opportunity to present a piece of prose that supports the theme of the poems which follow.

Note: The account provided actually happened. I was with a work group on assignment in Baumholder, Germany. The four of us had taken a field trip; a hike into the near-by forest. It is was an enchanted place; interspersed with medieval castle ruins, and remnants of an earlier Celtic settlement. One member of the group, and I split from the group, and went off on our own to explore a ruin...

We climbed a crumbling stone walkway to the castle ruin. From the court yard at the top we could see a vast green sward below us. The spirit of the past which inhabits these ancient places is palpable. You can feel a presence as if the ghosts of the Saxons still resided there, and continue to carry on their commerce, wage their wars and live their lives as they had eight hundred years ago. I became aware that my colleague was studying me intently, as if trying to remember something that had eluded her. "What is it?" I asked. "You okay? You look like you've seen a ghost."

"Maybe I have. Close your eyes and be quiet and very still. And tell me what you see."

I didn't question her. I did what she asked...and...

I see a man and a woman. And I am that man. I am wearing an armor breastplate. It surprises me that I know it is called a cuirass. I'm attempting to dismantle it. I'm tired, hurt, and the armor is weighing me down. There is a woman dancing in the field. Her eyes are closed and she does not notice me approach her. Her garments are flowing with her graceful movements as she turns in a gyring fashion; her arms out-stretched like a ballet dancer. Her hair is swirling like golden strands of spun gossamer. She doesn't yet see me. I'm almost close enough to touch her. I don't want to startle her, but I desperately need her help. The ties of the breastplate are along my spine, and beyond my reach. My hip is on fire with pain. I look at my right hip and I see the broken shaft of an arrow. It's buried deep, and I think it's penetrated my pelvic bone. The arrow has pierced the fauld which is supposed to protect my waist and hips. There is a thin rivulet of blood running the length of my right leg. It has soaked the armored sabaton that covers my foot. I feel lightheaded, and can no longer stand and bear the weight on my right side. The lady sees me. She is shocked to see that a man has come upon her, and that he is in shambles from a battle in which he did not fare well. She is angry with herself that she wasn't on her guard against this intrusion. Her mortification is brief. Her attention becomes focused on my wounds and shattered visage. She approaches me tentatively; with both cautiousness and compassion. She supports my arm which has grown slack and hangs by my side. I feel as though the sky is a pressing stone intent on crushing me beneath its weight. I go down on my knees, making every effort to remain up-right. I see a lovely face that must be the angel of heaven come to take me to my Savior. An awful darkness engulfs me and I feel cold as if buried beneath an avalanche of snow. And then…there is nothing.

"Now what happens? Go on."

"There's nothing else. Every thing's dark."

"Keep your eyes closed. Mine are closed too. Just watch…"

I'm off-balanced with what's just happened. With what I saw, or more like it, had just experienced. The vision sent a shock through me as if I had been jolted by a thousand joules of current through my heart. I really didn't want to repeat the experience, but I am intrigued at the same time. I am curious as to why this is happening to me. And what role, if any, this friend plays. It seems as though she acts as a catalyst for a powerful reaction that has me boiling with old and familiar images and feelings. **I shut my mind off, and**...

I am an old man. There is the vestige of a younger man still in love with this wizened face looking down at me. Her face is a map of wrinkles like a tea strained map pointing the way to a buried treasure. Her eyes are a deep green; still youthful in their emerald clarity. They are both beautiful and sad. I am listening to her tale. She is telling me a story – of us – so that I will take the memories to the life beyond this one. I must be dying because I am weak; deeply weary with a cold I feel in my bones. I'm not able to speak or rise from this hard pallet on which I lie supine with advancing rigor. I can communicate with her only with my eyes. I feel a rising panic like seeing a far off tidal wave moving toward me gathering great speed and I unable to move. She calms my panic with a stroke of her hand as she brushes my cheek and hushes me in a gentle, soothing way.

'You came into my life with little spirit left in you from wounds suffered in battle. You nearly died. I and my Lord's surgeon nursed you back to this life. My lord – my husband then – was not pleased with the attention I gave you, because I believe he knew the future of our instant bond. When finally you bedded me in the forest glade amidst the lupine and the green grass, our passion only grew. It came to pass that we could not conceal our admiration for each other. My husband's spies saw us climb the glacis; my hand in yours. Although I lied and told my lord it was for support as the embankment was steep and my foothold unsure, he punished me and banished you from our lands. The scars on my back are from the lashes

administered by the nuns while my lord watched. Not another word of you was spoken. I knew not where you had gone or if you still lived. I surely believed that my lord's huntsmen had killed you and left you for the wolves. And here you lie in this castle chamber dying, and I am here again by your side - this time to say goodbye. My lord has been gone for many years and I searched for you all this time. I do not regret that I have found you at last, and I do not grieve the lost years without you, although I will mourn your passing. We will meet again, my love. May the gods unite us again, and bless our love to last. Goodbye my dying knight...'

I am embarrassed that tears are running down my cheeks when I open my eyes. My friend is full of sadness as well. She takes both of my hands in hers. She tells me what she saw, and it was the same as what I had experienced... We walked back in silence...And did not speak of it again.

A classical theme set in a fairy tale? A man having child-like fantasies cast with medieval maidens, satyrs and fauns? Had the dream been a woman's, would it have cast unicorns and fairies? Possibly. Who cares? I have had other dreams such as these, though far darker. There have been women in them whose role it seems were there to comfort me in the final hours of my life. I once envisioned myself riding a mount through a forest; my body slouched on the mounts bareback. I had been riding through rain for days, and I was sick, chilled and exhausted. I was wearing buckskins that were impregnated with grease to repel the rain, yet I was soaked through to the skin. My lungs burned as if I were still inhaling hot cinders from a campfire grown cold, and reduced to wet ashes days ago. My ride terminated before a Hogan inhabited by an Indian woman. She cared for me by the warmth of her fire, but

I died after being shortly in her care. And that was it. It was painful to experience the vision. It was as if I were re-experiencing the sickness and death that I had envisioned.

If I were to interpret this vision with others in its category, I would say I have mother issues. My own mother gave birth to me under an extreme condition of toxemia. I came into the world under protest, and was met by a mother who was likewise unhappy and unwell. Though she looked after me and cared for me nonetheless. 'Eureka!' I might exclaim. That's it. That's what these dreams represent. Maybe.

In a final gesture of sharing, I will recount one other. It is brief. It was a shocking image which arose in the stillness of a quiet meditation. No mother figure here. No fairy tale theme. Just stark and poignant.

I sit with eyes closed; having repositioned my cramped legs after an unsuccessful lotus sitting posture. Now, all's dark and still. I've always liked being separated from the busy world out there. An opportunity to leave it for awhile is a luxury. However appearing before me on a rocky outcropping on a vaguely familiar sea shore is a seated skeleton, draped in a tattered long coat. It bears German military insignias on the collars. Around the man-of-bones neck are campaign ribbons hung like garland on a parched Christmas tree. A boney finger crookedly points in my direction. It is barely attached to an arm whose ulna and radius are broken and splintered, and from which black decayed marrow is exposed. Lovely image, huh?

So, enough about my dreams. How about yours? If you're not inclined to share them with anyone but your therapist, fine. Read on, and let the dreams go on. May only your grandest dreams come true.

Dreams

"We grow great by dreams. All big men are dreamers. They see things in the soft haze of a spring day or in the red fire of a long winter's evening. Some of us let these great dreams die, but others nourish and protect them; nurse them though bad days till they bring them to the sunshine and light which comes always to those who sincerely hope that their dreams will come true."   § Woodrow Wilson

Waking up In Dreams

Dreaming Self:

Did I dream of you,
And wake to find you gone?
As I lie in bed,
Tangled in,
The rumpled sheets,
That I embrace,
Pretending that it's you,
Who hide from me,
Behind the veil,
Of a summer night's,
Dream?

Did I dream,
This strand of yellow hair,
Wrapped around my finger,
Like Coleridge's flower,
Plucked from,
Heaven's meadow,
While he dreamt,
And woke up with it,
In his hand?

Haven't I seen you,
Many nights before,
And didn't I embrace you,
In the flesh,
The scent of you,
Still clinging to me,
The morning after,
When I woke,
Reminding me of,
The wisteria,
Blooming,
Just Outside,
My window?

Why do you vanish,
With the sunrise,
Yet appear,
Under the light,
Of the gibbous moon,
So real to me?
Playing tricks,
Like some,
Blithe spirit,
Teasing me,
With your fairy,
Mischief.

You are real,
I insist,
And so am I,
To you,
In all the dreams,
We've shared.

I can always,
Hear,
Your parting words:
"Until we meet again,"
When I am still,
Groggy,
And grains of sand,
Invade the corners,
Of my eyes…
Evidence of,
The dusty roads,
And the fields,
Of grass,
And sand,
On which we,
Walked,
And played.

Waking Self:

Am I dreaming you,
Who lies beside me,
When I wake up,
From the dream?

You...
Whose raven hair,
Is fanned out,
Across the pillow,
The scent of you,
Still ripe,
With lusty,
Adventures,
Partaken,
By you,
In your dream.

Who did you court
With whom you have,
A History,
And relationship,
No less real,
For the logic,
And events,
Unevenly,
Sequential,

In our,
Ever so creative,
And forgiving minds?

Though,
It should not,
Matter,
That you and I,
Enter separately,
The theater,
Of our deep,
Unconscious sleep,
You dare insist...
It does.

Jealous of lives,
Oh, yes,
Of the same substance,
Yet of different form,
That you argue,
Are the same,
Because...
We have,
A gift,
That makes,
Our wishes,
Real,

Carelessly mocking,
The waking love,
We share.

I dare you,
To cease dreaming,
And enter,
The empty,
Place,
Which lies between,
The sleep
And waking dream,
Where in the darkness,
We are absent,
Gone!
Like a candle,
Flame,
Extinguished by,
A breeze.

Being freed,
From life's,
Rough and gentle,
Turnings,

And grieving,
The missing,
Rapture,
And the danger,
Of our,
Double lives.

I am willing
To straddle,
The Limn,
Of both worlds,
And become,
A lucid dreamer,
And a lucid waker,
If that means,
Having both of you,
Separate,
And ubiquitous,
Out of my own,
Free will,
Only possible,
If I can write,
The scripture.

Your free will,
May project upon,
The screen,
Of your creation,
Editions,

That we share,
Like sculptors,
Collaborating,
On a work,
Each applying clay,
To some vague form,
Wielding all
The powers,
Of our,
Manifestation,
And yielding detail,
To the common,
Vision,
That we share.

I bring to you,
This morning,
The cup,
From which,
My dream lover,
And I drank,
Before I woke,
Filled,
To the same measure,
As before,
As if no other,
Lover's lips,
Had touched it,

Held only in my hands,
And carved by me,
In detail,
Suffused with symbols,
Of pure imagination,
Whose meaning,
You will learn,
From the dreams,
This cup's potion,
Will induce.

Drink!
As my dream lover,
Had,
The sweet libation,
From this cup,
Its lip carved deep,
With twisting,
Flowered tendrils,
And the,
Blood-red fruit,
Of Ivy.

Let us twist,
And turn,
Entwined as lovers,
In an old,
Relationship,
In each,
New dream...
Renewed.

Dreaming Self:

Did I dream of you?
And wake to find you gone?
As I lie in bed,
Tangled in,
The rumpled sheets,
That I embrace,
Pretending that it's you,
Who hide from me,
Behind the veil,
Of a winter night's,
Dream?

Did I dream,
This strand of raven hair,
Wrapped around my finger,
Like Coleridge's flower,
Plucked from,
Heaven's meadow,
While he dreamt,
And woke up with it,
In his hand?

Fire and Ashes

My world had burned,
To ashes,
Before I met you,
I had lit the fire,
And torched,
Dry tinder hearts,
Bursting into flame,
Too easy,
To ignite,
So eager,
To destroy,
The need.

Too ready...
Too inflammable,
To have brought,
The torch,
So near,
So shameful,
That I placed,
Still beating hearts,
Upon the,
Funeral pyre.

How wicked of you,
To come along,
And,
Douse,
The embers,
∞
While,
I waited,
For,
The rain,
∞
That,
Would have,
Washed,
The ashes,
Clean.

How wicked of you,
To deny,
A destiny,
∞
That would,
Have,
Let me,
Start,
Again,
∞
Or end,
The game,
I've played.

A barrow,
Would,
Have made,
A cozy bed,
∞
And,
A good,
Resting place,
∞
To lay,
My ashes,
Down.

How wicked of you,
To wake me up,
And make me,
Play your game,
∞
Pretending,
I am living,
Once again,
∞
Because you,
Told me,
That you,
Love me.

How wicked,
Was,
My former lover,
To have,
Lied to me,
∞
Telling me,
That she never,
Felt that way,
 ∞
And that I,
Brought her,
Nothing,
But heartbreak,
And pain.

How very wicked,
Is she now,
That she,
Has risen,
From the ashes,
 ∞
Saying that I,
Called her forth,
To give her,
One last chance,
To love,
Again,

∞
After…
I,
Found,
You.

How very blessed,
Am I,
To live among,
The wicked,
Who will,
Help me,
Love again,
∞
When I must,
Chance,
More seasons,
Of draught,
And…
The risk,
Of,
Burning up,
Again!

Rather it,
Be fire,
Than,
Whither,
To dry,
Husk,

∞
Caused,
By,
Our own,
Benign,
Neglect.
∞
Or by,
Damming up,
The river,
That feeds,
The warm,
Gulf,
Waters…
∞
Into which,
We used,
To wade,
To briefly,
Ease,
The,
Chill.

What do I do,
That I have you:
Two lovers…
To make me,
New again,

∞

When both of you,
Seduced me,
∞
Into,
Playing,
Such,
A wicked,
Game?

I am wicked too,
And I will play the game,
Hoping it is real,
Though until I know,
For sure,
I'll dip the brand,
In oil,
And keep,
My flint,
And steel.

Promise me,
You will not keep,
So distant,
Even,
If you should,
Feel,
The burn,

∞
And I,
Will keep,
My promise,
∞
And vow,
To,
Do,
The,
Same.

Izmir Bazaar

Like a dreamer,
I walk,
The crowded streets,
And explore,
The maze of alleys,
In the bazaar,
Of Kameralti,
Izmir,
Where he 17th century,
Is now,
And forever near!
My senses assailed,
By an aromatic tide,
That floods,
The cinnamon,
And chili pepper,
Regions of my brain.

Oh, sweet,
And bitter,
Effleurage,
Of the ancient,
And the modern,
Musk,
Of busy trade,
And sweat,
Of human toil,
Causing a rush,
That excites,

A deep historic
Recognition,
In my olfactory,
Memory!

The ember,
Of Kameralti,
Burns hotly,
In the Central Mosque,
I, standing in slippers,
Among the Islamic faithful,
Who gathered there,
When the adhan called.
Here in a thurible,
Of warm pressed flesh,
Anointed with jasmine,
And a sea,
Of moist breath,
Flavored with,
Clove tobacco,
Exhaled,
Into the streets,
In the smoky,
Fog of,
Commerce.

Springtime in Kameralti,
Is carried,
On the currents,
Of the sirocco wind,
Saturated with,
The biting sands,
Of the Western desert.
Relentlessly scouring,
The leaden dust,
From cracked stone,
And mosaic courtyards,
Rising to spread,
Its glaucous wings,
To chase away,
The cold specter,
Of winter,
Through,
Labyrinthine streets.

I hear the winds,
And the prayers,
From the masjed,
Keening shrilly,
In the manner,
Of excited Moslem women,
Gathered in the square.

Along the Anafartalar,
Caddesi,
I see whirling Dervishes,
Of paper and trash,
Whipped up,
By a breeze...
Racing to the square,
To perform under arches,
Of twisted grape root,
Waiting to bloom.

And men...
Impatient with,
The dust and sweat,
Which cakes their feet,
Gather 'round,
The fountain,
Of Donertas Sebili,
To indulge,
In their ablution.

I sit among them,
Resting on a stool,
Feet cooling,
Under a faucet,
Of running water,
In a community,
Of craggy toes,
And wrinkled feet,

Cleansing me,
Of my prejudices,
And filling me up,
With the wisdom,
Of silence,
And the music,
Of the Tambour.

With clean skin,
And clear eyes,
From the hub,
Of a marble fountain,
In the square,
I behold the spokes,
On which has slowly,
Turned the wheel,
Of progress,
Not so hurried here,
No fancy stalls,
Or orderly shelves,
Stocked,
With modern goods,
Though swept,
And dusted daily,
And patrolled,
By packs,
Of hungry,
Feral cats.

What rushes to,
My eyes,
Is our world,
Seen,
Through the fractal beauty,
Of a stained glass window,
Broken into splintered shards,
Like a puzzle,
Of the thousand places,
I have traveled,
Shaken in a box,
And tossed in Kameralti's,
Tessellated alleys,
Overflowing with Persian,
And Egyptian wares,
And brick-a-bract,
From all the corners,
Of the world.

Not to mention,
Leather and kilims,
Fruits and vegetables,
Nuts, and baklava,
Raki, fish,
And olive oil,
Redolent,
And malodorous,

As rank,
As the stink,
Of the sewer,
And as sweet,
As the scent,
Of perfume,
Confusing my senses;
Wishing I had extra-
Added receptors,
To codify,
And sample,
Them all!

I move with a caravan,
Of shoppers,
Dodging,
Aggressive merchants,
Who prey upon,
The tourist
They take me for.
I do not want,
A leather jacket,
After buying soap,
Or meet the cousin,
Of the soap merchant,
Who Sells,
Water pipes.

I buy a string,
Of prayer beads,
And a Turkish cap,
And wear dark shades,
To hide blue eyes,
To blend in with,
The Greek,
The Turk,
A Levantine,
Or an Armenian Jew,
And I succeed,
In browsing one day,
Unmolested,
Not being led,
By the arm,
To meet a brother,
Selling Turkish carpets,
After drinking tea.

The Kapali Carsi
The Chamber of Dreams

I wait at the Carsikapi gate,
Of the Grand Bazaar,
Of historic Istanbul,
And I...
Hesitate to enter,
(So unlike me).

I know that when,
The gate opens,
Luring us to the calls,
Of the merchants'
Daily commerce,
That there,
Will be memories,
Lurking there,
As ubiquitous,
As midnight shadows,
Running from the pale moon,
Under which I slept,
And dreamt,
The night before.

I wake to the dream.
Of yesterday,
And rediscover,
Plentiful wares,
Exhumed from their,
Cavernous bedestens,
And stacked along,
The covered streets,
Fifty-eight in all,
Like the axon hillocks,
Running the avenues,
Of my busy brain.
And on whose course,
There are crossroads,
Blind alleys,
And dead-ends,
Which begin some place,
And end nowhere.

But also….
There are treasured,
Memories to be found,
Though hidden,
From me,
In vast repositories,
Not always…
Willfully recollected,
Like the memories,

That I had nearly…
Forgotten…
Of her.

She is here…
Following me,
From a safe distance,
And whose presence I sense,
Among the gallimaufry,
Of useless things,
Like the *flow*,
Of an acid trip,
Whose coherence,
I do not yet realize.

She is not,
To be lost,
Among the masses,
Who stroll these,
Tacky thoroughfares,
Or lost in the distraction,
Of the congeries,
Of Silk, and gold,
And spice,
For she is the one,
True precious thing,
That I have nearly lost,
In the crowd,

Yet who shines brightly,
Even amidst,
The glittering farrago,
Of richly over-valued goods.

I did not meet her here,
But I am with her,
In ways that are like,
A waking dream,
In which I am trapped.
And like a paralytic,
Wrapped in staves,
I cannot extend my reach,
To give a hug.
I struggle hard,
Against my bonds,
In this desperate dream,
From which I hope to wake,
And still find you there.

I met you in,
The Tropic of Cancer,
In the heat,
Of a Florida summer,
Where our love once burned,
As hot as a plasma storm,
Generated by the sun,

So quick it was,
To fuse our flesh as one,
How long,
To scorch our hearts,
And see them,
Cool to ash?

We travelled far,
And lived in foreign places,
Alien to our tongues,
And unfamiliar to our customs,

We walked more roads,
Than Kapali Carsi's,
Myriad alleyways,
And lit more candles,
In cathedrals,
And bowed our heads,
In more mosques,
As we passed through,
More carriage gates,
Than all of Istanbul,
Could offer.

A solitary traveler,
Is at risk,
For hazards,
On the road,
He sets upon to walk,

And when taking lodging,
In the desolation,
Of a dark and cramped,
Cold Inn.

He dreams of keeping company,
With mischief,
Tempted by the vacuity,
Of a heart and soul,
In awful disrepair,
Swayed by apparitions,
Of youthful chorus girls,
Wearing silver,
Halter tops,
Whose bodies dance with grace,
In see-through cotton skirts,
Singing to strophes,
That do not scan,
To the haunting music,
Of the Baglama.

The dream of Kapali Carpi,
Is where I woke,
Having sought to,
Find you there,
Hidden so well,
That I could not see,
You standing,
So boldly there,
In front of me.

I heard,
The song sirvente,
Of a strolling,
Ghostly minstrel,
Whose words,
Were whispers,
Loud enough to call,
To life,
My brazen,
Stubborn heart,
Found wandering,
In the trickster's
Illusion of a dream,
And waking me,
To sweet memories,
Of so long ago,
To remind me,
How to…
Love you,
Once again.

Nature

Every so many years, we reinvent ourselves, as we must in order to live among the moderns. We were originally invented in the dreams our parents had about us. In the dreams of our awakened spirit, we must accomplish this routinely; over and over on our own.

∞ The Author

The Mariner's Course
Part I

I had studied the sailing charts,
That insisted that,
The world was flat,
And I corrected the fallacy,
Discovering the unknown truth,
At seemingly great risk.
Because I did not fall,
Into the Great Abyss,
Guarded by the Leviathan,
At the edge of my map.

I leave deep waters,
To discover the New World,
For the Old one I left behind,
Dwells among the ghosts,
Of faded memory,
The definitions of its boundaries,
Long since shifted and eroded,
Like the miles of sandy beaches,
Devoured by the seasons,
And the tides.

I now leave foot prints,
Where before,
I left ripples in the currents,
Of the eighteen seas and oceans,
Which tug at the hem of dry land.

I am determined,
To seek a life,
And in finding it,
Discover a loving companion,
Should the improbable,
Be realized,
Much less reconciled,
In so short a time,
Within my generation.

This is the course I've set,
That nothing will deter,
Unless the ground beneath my feet,
Opens up and swallows me,
Or some serendipity of fate,
Cuts shorter my time,
Among the living.

The path on land,
Though fraught with its own dangers,
Diversions,
And distractions,
Seems surer,
And more solid,
To the peripatetic traveler.

Less chance I take,
The stakes less steep,
On stable terra firma.

More drastic is the fate,
That waits beneath,
A liquid veil,
So thin.

Comprised of,
Simple molecules,
No more substantial,
Than the mixture of the air,
I breathe,
And so eager to drown,
The reckless and the careless.

No change in the prevailing wind,
Will slow my will's momentum,
No bay that hosts a fickle tide,
Will cause variations in direction.

Though I have always,
Been methodical,
And trust unequivocally,
In more rational methods,
When searching,
For fulfillment…

In spite of others,
Who might say,
'This way ignores the importance,
Of the heart's involvement.'

What do these native people know?
The same ones I encountered,
Long ago.

How much better now?
For the millennia,
That it took,
To learn,
To walk upright,
And fashion tools,
Which doubled soon,
As weapons.

Not much more than this,
Have we evolved!

We are the cause,
Of our misfortunes,
Having labeled virtues,
Like kindness,
And compassion...
Weakness.

Waging wars,
And never finished,
With the slaughter,
Still trading lives,
Of the innocent,
For profit.

Insatiable is our appetite,
For consumption,
This very well,
Could be,
My own projection.

Part II

Starting over...

I will go back,
And find the life,
Which rose from the murkiness,
Of the coal-dark regions,

Taking eons,
To ascend.
Before coming,
To rest,
In the pelagic cradle.

Where sunshine pierced holes,
And made eyes,
For the hideous, sightless creatures,
To bear witness,
To the splendors made possible,
In the organic regions,
Of the earth's fertile mantel.

Fed I am told,
By complex ratios,
Of atmospheric gases,
And liquids rich in nutrients,
Made of a briny slurry,
Of stinking mud,

The scent of boiling sulfur,
And decay,
Then, pounded out,
In a crucible,
With a pestle,
Hewn from pillars of granite.
And fired in the kiln,
Of the sun.

Its furious heat ,
Creating composites,
Of brand new matter,
More fragile than glass,
No more substantial,
Than flaccid muscle,
And sagging hide,
Held together by struts,
Of brittle calcium.

I now comb the littorals,
Wading in the shallows,
Of the salt water marshes,
That encircle,
A hundred million miles,
Of coastline once pristine,
Now polluted and ready,
For another evolution.

I steer a course,
Far from the Continental Shelves,
And deliberately avoid,
The Midnight zones,
Rather mapping my course,
For some beach head or sub littoral,
One conducive to fashioning,
A new life,
In the manner of an alchemist,
Determined to turn dull lead,
To precious gold.

I find instead,
The basic elements,
Of what I am made.

Only heaped up piles,
Of chalk-white powder.

Diatomaceous earth,
Riddled with the skeletons,
Of single celled creatures,
Returned from the barren,
Benthic landscapes,
Of former oceans,
To inhabit the vast deserts,
And empty salt flats.

Insistent rains,
And scorching heat,
Turns the wondrous clay,
From which God,
Made Adam
Into alabaster.

Absent is the spark,
Required to ignite,
The spirit.
Exiguous and reviled,
As useless,
As coprolite,
Gathered from chamber pots,
Unearthed in Pompeii.

And as solid as the wicked,
Turned to Salt,
In Sodom and Gomorrah.

I have encountered,
Ghastly white amputees,
Skulking through,
The wilderness,
And have climbed hills,
Of crusted sandstone,
Resembling habitats,

Deceptive in their beauty,
Reminding me,
Of lost cities,
Like Babylon, and Samara,
Long ago abandoned,
And crumbled into ruin.

Now, dead and desiccated,
Home to disembodied spirits,
And frozen marble statuary,
Staring vacantly,
Through blind eyes,
In time- worn faint relief.

I would that I could,
Meet little Lucy,
Recently arrived,
From Ethiopia,
With skin the color,
Of the beaten hide,
Of an African shield.

More likely,
I shall meet,
A Nordic princess,
Whose complexion,
Once youthful,
Is now before me,

Aged like cracqueleur,
Threaded through a globe,
Of antique ivory.

This is the inevitable course-
Of youth,
Of novelty,
And beauty.

What essential powers do I lack,
To make a just and good companion,
Or simply pour one,
From a flask of human chemistry,
To birth one upon a shore,
So rich in the promise of a new life,
And one so full of possibilities?

Searching this vast shore,
For living company that is new,
Novel and original,
Has been sadly uneventful.

I would be content,
To make companion,
Of the lifeless or the wicked.

Rather this,
Than be alone,
Last living man,
To walk upon,
The earth.

Beauty may be present,
And life accounted for,
In the stillness of a moment,
Not much planned.

Not up ahead,
To be found,
Not far behind,
To be rediscovered.

Perhaps it is a life,
Of shared moments,
And omnipresent history.

Not memories,
Tied to strings,
Wound tight,
Around a finger,
To remember,
Or joined by bands,
Of precious metal,
Sensitive to changes,
In the weather.

Part III

Life...

Not like that which crawled to shore,
From the sunlit realm,
Of the ocean's womb,
(And lies hidden from me,
In the shadows).

Rather,
That which was there all along,
The very one,
Who shared this life,
And walked invisibly,
Beside me.

Less the intrepid adventurer, I,
More dishonest,
With my axiomatic habit,
Of covering the truth,
With lies.

For searching often blinds,
The seeker,
Who misses what is near,
While looking far away.

I held the sailor's glass to peer,
Beyond my senses.

It was not missing,
From the places I had been,
Nor was it waiting,
At my destinations,
It was not waiting,
To be made by me,
Out of the globigerina ooze,
That collected in the tidal pools,
Along the shore.

It had always walked,
Beside me,
In luminescent form,
Dissipating in the day,
And hiding,
In the shadows,
Of the night.

It followed me everywhere,
And was always there,
Though I did not see it,
Nor did I reach out to touch it,
Or take it by the hand,
Or hold it in love's embrace.

How near the companion,
That we seek,
And keep perpetually,
Beyond a reach,
That does not exceed,
Even half a fathom.

How simple,
Are the things,
We complicate.

How toxic,
Is the lie.

How ephemeral,
Is the precious thing,
We seek.

How permanent,
The precious thing,
We find.

Joshua Tree

My Joshua Tree,
Is the solitary sentry,
Of the south Mogollon Rim,
That guards the peaceful solitude,
Of the high Mojave Desert.

My Joshua Tree,
Stands straight,
Like Twisted Hair,
Coarse and dry,
And tied,
With prickly cactus twine.
Named erroneously,
By Mormons -
Their Joshua,
With arms outstretched,
Before the Promised Land.

Thinking as aliens would,
That just set foot,
Upon a barren planet,
So vastly different,
From their own,
As if Moses' successor,
Could be so blind.

My Joshua Tree,
Is no Aramaic lunatic,
Driven mad by thirst,
Or hungering for sand,
Mistaking it for manna.

I see the Joshua Tree,
From my Mount Pisgah.
I have even seen god,
A time or two,
When I was parched,
And famished.
Shimmering in the mirage,
While he strolled,
Along the mesa,
At high noon.

My Joshua Tree,
Could, by some harsh fate,
Become a burning bush,
Ignited into flame,
By Mormon-hating miners,
Seeking to immolate,
Some wayward Joshua,
To feed the insatiable,
Slag fires,
To reveal,
The shining ore.

My Joshua Tree,
Could, by some harsh fate,
Become dead,
Fence posts,
Made of the bones,
Of its trunks and branches,
Mutilated by farmers,
Who sought to spur,
The growth of progress,
In the stillness,
Of this vast desert.

My Joshua Tree,
Has planted itself,
By wretched gulches,
Near promised waters,
That fill dry beds,
Of desert rivers,
After rain.

My Joshua Tree,
How does it know,
Where to be,
That it can thrive,
A hundred years or more?

On this depends,
The generosity,
Of the moth,
And the devilment,
Of the weevil,
Entangled in a twisted fate,
Whose given name they share.

My Joshua Tree's,
Time on earth,
It is not measured,
In the graceful tempo,
Of cyclical life and death,
But in the two-step,
Simple rhythm,
Of precarious,
Give and take.

My Joshua Tree,
It seems to age like me,
That once walked,
Briskly through,
Fertile valleys,
And now stands still,
Upon this patch of ground,
Ignoring the pain,
Of bloodless cuts,
That score cracked heals,
Planted in the dust.

My Joshua Tree,
And I,
Await the monsoons,
Of the Spring,
To flood this,
Hollow gully we have chosen,
And overflow,
And nourish,
In the lotic streams,
The Joshua Tree and me.

My Joshua Tree,
And I,
Will be replenished,
From the root-base,
Of our natures,
Filling us to the level,
That life requires,
Sufficient to encourage,
The dormant bloom,
And slake an aching thirst.

My Joshua Tree,
And I,
Await another summer,
That will invite,
More time,
To feast upon,
The cactus pear,
And the nectar,
Of the bees.

On the Lighter Side

Pulp Fiction

I create the heroes of Fiction,
Printed on pulp,
Cheap paper,
That feels rough,
Like the coarseness,
Of a wash woman's hands.

Pulp,
Cheap paper,
Sent through the beater,
Pressed between the jack,
Slipped into the drying rack,
Wrung dry.

Paper,
Cheap paper,
Inked up with stories,
Appealing to the mass market,
Telling tales of murder and mayhem,
Of vixens, and villains...
Oh my!

Stories,
Appealing stories,
Tickling imaginations,
Like the wash woman's hands,
Stroking the sensitive,
Parts of her man.

Put the part,
The sensitive part of you,
Between softer pages of vellum,
And imagine the vixen,
Not the wash woman,
Tickling your…
Vivid imagination.

I am a writer of pulp fiction,
I play to your subliminal instincts,
Sordid, dirty, grimy,
Deliciously naughty…
As you like it,
And so do I.

Poet

Poetry?
Oh, come on!
Pretty prose,
Set to some meter,
That makes me count,
Makes me crazy,
Like listening to,
The Queen's English,
Instead of strident Yankee,
Making me think rhyming words,
Figuring how to spell
Words that are onomatopoeia,
What the hell!

Can't get straight,
To the point?
The way I drink Tequila.
Straight up.
No...o!
Poetry is a Margarita.
Taking my Tequila,
Turning it into the nectar,
Of the prickly mescal cactus,
Surviving like a hero,
In the harsh Sonora desert,
Like a Mexican illegal,
On the Devil's deathly Highway.

Hear what I'm saying?
Yes?
Pretty enough to the ears,
Though my tongue and gut,
Don't really care that much,
Just piss colored hooch,
Cool to the touch,
Warming my innards,
Inspiring me to eloquence,
More often though,
Incoherence.

Maybe I'll order the Margarita,
Seeking poetry,
By drinking one.
For mighty sour,
Is the Persian lime,
Pretty tasty with Cointreau,
Exciting my dull sense of taste,
With distillations,
Of the peel of sweet and bitter oranges,
Sweetened with the sugar,
Of the beet.

Just an ounce,
Of the secret family recipe,
Of brothers Adolphe and Edouard-Jean Cointreau,
It wouldn't taste as good,
I suppose
If made from Indian River oranges,
By Adolf and Ed,
Behind their tool shed?

My poetic cocktail,
Is incomplete without,
The right glass with salt around the rim,
What is a poem if not shaped like an hour glass?
Neatly framed upon the page,
Well sort of like this one,
Although it bulges here and there,
Like love handles on a fat man.
But this is poetry,
Slender and precise,
Fitted neat upon the page,
And metered in two-step marching time,
At a pace to slow the band,
Some sappy skip-to-my-Lou,
Treacle sweet,
Like two-parts Remy Cointreau.

Screw this love of sweet refrains,
Of Fairy-dance and buttercups,
Of sugary drinks,
And pretty, pretty prose.
Skip the sheer beach cover-up,
Bend over in your thong,
Don't skip though golden meadows,
Do the bars crawl down Duval.

Pour me Jose Cuervo Especial,
Piss-colored eighty-proof,
And I will drink to thee.
I'll extemporize a verse or two,
That I will dedicate to you,
But promise me you'll do one thing,
If I become,
Romantic,
Purple or bromidic…
Just tell me to shut the hell up,
And stop writing,
Poetry.

Flesh & Blood

Beauty & Mathematics

"There is nothing like dream to create the future. Utopia to-day, flesh and blood tomorrow."

§ Victor Hugo, *Les Miserables,1862*

Immortal Me

I am bound to live forever,
If I can stay put,
In the moment,
Because in the parsed phrase,
Of a minute,
Which I'll further explain,
In a moment,
Is much more,
Than a minute,
Making a minute,
An infinite number,
Of moments–
Take my word for it.

If this is double-talk,
So be it,
Because double-talk,
Tripled, quadrupled,
Multiplied ad infinitum,
Is, well, redundant,
Stretching the point…
Beyond anyone's comprehension,
Like some mathematical
Exponential,
As in 10,
To the power of,
A hundred (10_{100}) .

Mathematics and Science,
Have collaborated,
To invent methods,
For a life everlasting.

Like *Time* itself,
As an Imperial measure,
Of the Metric,
Proposing to expand time,
Beyond the short-lived
Standard,
Of limited,
Unit conversion.

Believe me when I say,
You should count your days,
In minutes, seconds and moments,
Not years,
Because a Mean Solar minute,
Is longer than,
A Sidereal one,
Except when,
Converting seconds,
To calendar years –
Don't ask.

You say, what difference does,
A miniscule fraction make?
Well, it's huge.
It's eighty-six thousand,
One hundred and seven,
Point fifteen more seconds,
a year.

I want every one of them,
Even more than,
I was born to have,
For each moment times that,
Is an inestimable amount,
Which, in case you don't know it,
Is a lot.

Medicine is determined,
To discover a potion,
Akin to the fabled waters,
Of the Fountain of Youth,
Anti-aging, anti-oxidants,
Along with a peptide,
Memory-enhancing,
Pharmaceutical brew,
Which I eagerly await,
Because I want to be,
As good - no better -
Than new!

Meditating in the moment,
Surpasses huge,
Mathematical calculations,
Which can be,
Further exceeded,
By 60'spsychedelics,
And anti-aging prescriptions,
Through whose powers,
I'll succeed in,
Becoming immortal-
At least for the moment!

I meditate in Metric Time,
Where days of 10 hours exist,
And hours are one-hundred,
Minutes apiece,
Times that by,
Its indivisible moments,
And well, as you know by now,
That's a lot.

There's a big deal raging,
About the nanosecond,
And it's sister, technology,
Applied to computers and lasers.

(Those practically invisible dimensions,
Fusing information and time,
Poised on a,
Non-localized platform,
Of seemingly,
Empty space)

Exactly the *place* I go,
When I meditate.

So what's the big deal?
How about the femto,
The apto,
And the zeptosecond,
And the biggest daddy,
Of them all -
The yocto...second.

Now there's a concept,
To consider:
That is,
Just increase,
The method,
Of counting,
And slow down,
The tempo of time,
For in their exponentials,
Dwell the ghosts,
Of all the tenses,
Of time.

Take this,
Times the moments,
And what have you got?
Hickory Dickory, Dock,
A mouse up a clock,
That takes forever,
And ever,
To strike… One -
Sorry!

In the meditative moment,
I travel by light years,
Across ten million miles,
No longer using,
The primitive abacus,
To keep track,
Of my earthly,
Borrowed time.

If you pondered this riddle,
That makes no sense at all,
Than you've squandered,
The five minutes,
It took to be read.

That's exactly three-hundred,
Mean Solar seconds,
And if measured,
In moments,
Is a hell of a...

Long time!

1.618

Behold the Beauty,
That is Phi,
Whose golden mean,
Determines who,
And what,
Is beautiful.

It shapes the eye,
And also the face,
In which,
Our window on the world,
Resides.

Nature's architect,
Designed every,
Living thing,
In our,
External world,
According to,
An elementary plan,
Scaled to One,
Point six,
One eight,

In a standard,
One scale,
Fits all,
Linear regularity,
That's called,
The Golden,
Phi.

After all…
How can we rely,
On unreliable,
And vague,
Inner transformations,
Calling something,
"Beautiful,"
That is governed,
By caprice,
And streaming bits,
Of light refracting,
Pixellations,
Playing first-run,
Flicks,
In the Dolby,
Digital,
Theater,
Of the,
Mind…

There must be,
So it's,
Generally believed,
By smarter men,
Than I,
That answers,
To the knotty questions,
Are to be found,
Beyond the boundaries,
Of the subjective,
Not arrived at,
By some,
Simple,
Uneducated,
Man,
In awe,
Over a,
Mere,
Sunset.

Whose idea was it anyway?
To write beauty's definition,
In a language,
None of us,
Can understand.

Phi is beautiful,
To the mathematician,
As is the ugly child,
Only to the mother,
Who keeps like company,
With some drooling,
Little monster,
Munching Gerber biscuits,
Like mathematicians,
Crunching numbers,
And drooling over,
Fibonacci numbers.

What is this,
Incoherent gibber,
That's oft,
Mistaken,
For some,
Telepathic language,
Of a distant,
Alien race,
Providing us,
With answers,
To hard questions;
Such as:
What is beauty?
Truth?
And Grace?

Convince me in writing,
Like The Ten Commandments do,
Carved in stone,
And delivered by,
The insured,
And bonded,
Messenger,
Of God.

Or write it in the language,
Of the new religion,
In which:
Math is Father,
Science the Son,
And Quantum Physics,
Is the Holy Ghost.

Oh yes, and,
Use strange glyphs:
And cipher,
Through the language,
Of applied mathematics,
Whose words spell, *Beauty*,
In letters,
That are circles,
Triangles,
And geometrical forms,
That lose me,
In the confusion,
Of their...

Oh so,
Elegant,
Symmetry.

But symmetry is beauty,
I am led to understand,
For in the well-proportioned,
Human form,
There is approximation,
Of perfection.

And in the combined features,
Of the ugly and the cute,
There is an average,
Which emerges,
That is better looking,
Than them both.

A pretty woman,
And an ugly man,
May not sire,
A kid-at-risk,
For a homely life alone,
But endow,
This lucky bastard,
With surprisingly,
Good looks!

It's a fact, you know,
That pretty people,
Earn more money,
And climb,
The corporate ladder,
Faster than others,
Less endowed;
Their handsomeness,
Defined in fine-boned,
Chiseled features,
Flawless,
Pink complexions,
And straight,
And shiny,
Hair.

I used to be,
Well, comfortable,
In the company,
Of very pretty people,
And thought that,
I was one of them,
Until I passed the mirror,
On the wall,
That told me,
Damn it?
I wasn't the fairest,
Of them all –
Not even close!

The awful truth,
This deprecating gaze,
Upon me,
Might reveal?
A most hideous object,
Of social avoidance,
And my love object's,
Curt rejection.
Not a chance,
That you will see me,
In the swimsuit issue,
Or a Calvin Kline...
Commercial.

Well, fuck them all,
For their short-sighted take,
Concerning what is pretty,
And what is not,
I am an ugly duckling,
Who'll grow up,
And still be...
An ugly duck,
No fairy tale ending,
Save for the Photoshop'ed me,
Posted on my Profile page,
On Face book.

If beauty is a gift,
From god,
Why is it,
If the gift's divine,
That it's dispensed,
Also to the wicked?
And great men,
Of sterling virtue,
Can be fashioned,
Into human clay,
That's lumpy,
And mis-shapened?

Socrates, and John Paul Sartre,
Gave us philosophies,
Their truths and revelations,
Immortal and Immutable,
The gifts they gave,
But hadn't gotten,
In return,
Aspiring to greatness,
In their works,
But not in looks,
Denied,
Their,
Equal,
Measure.

Lincoln was homely,
And careless of his looks,
In his carriage,
And his bearing,
He was sad,
Disheveled,
And depressed.

Melancholy dripped,
From him,
As he shuffled,
Through the crowds.

As a specimen,
He was atrocious,
As a Statesman,
He was profound,
Little comfort,
In the accolade,
For a man,
No gorgeous lady'd.
Keep around.

Don't insult me,
With a bromide,
Such as:
All beauty lies within,
That it's an elixir,
Composed of virtue,
Charisma,
Smarts,
And grace.

Rather, give me:
Youth,
And health,
And a graceful,
Symmetry,
Created by,
The Phi.

If beauty should be judged,
In the eye of the beholder,
Then stab it,
With a pointy stick,
And make the judges blind,
Not seeing,
My rough,
And unattractive,
Looks,
They'll, mistake me,
For,
Adonis.

I apologize,
For being unkind,
I was hoping,
That in being wicked,
I'd be rewarded.
You know,
Like going to bed,
And waking up…
Attractive.

[I'll mend my ways…]

I'll study,
The Indian Rasas,
In drama and in theory,
And become the ardent student,
Whose devotion,
Is rewarded,
With…
Everlasting,
Beauty.

I insist on,
Being selective though,
And accomplish only two:
So, I'll dance the Sangaram,
And the Hasyam too.

In the dance is manifested,
My most desired goals:
Transforming what is,
Ugly,
In physicality,
And mood,
To attractivess,
Most sought after,
Along with,
Laughter,
Love,
And,
Mirth.

I'll worship,
Vishnu and Pramata,
If they'll grant,
This wish,
For me,
I'm not ashamed,
For asking,
If nothing else,
I've tried.

I'm tired of chasing,
After beauty,
That runs,
Away,
From me,
And,
Hides.

I won't look for it,
In numbers,
I refuse,
To factor Phi,
I'll find it,
In all seasons,
Under cloudy skies,
And clear,
In the colors
Of the rainbow,
And in the smile,
Of every,
Child.

www.ingramcontent.com/pod-product-compliance
Lightning Source LLC
Chambersburg PA
CBHW031411040426
42444CB00005B/509